Our Journey

His Plan

By

Ophelia Ray

AARON PUBLISHING

Printed in the United States of America

First Printing, September 2018

ISBN 978-1-7324444-2-3

Published by

Aaron Publishing

PO Box 1144

Shelbyville, TN 37162

www.aaronpublishing.com

Foreword

I knew some time ago that Ophelia was writing down things she remembered from our ministry and how it began. It was a thrill when she shared what she had written with me and then asked me to write something about the book. After reading her finished product, I realized just how good she is at expressing herself through the written word. I knew the story because I lived it with her, but I was blown away by the deep insight she had into our ministry. She was able to see things that I had missed. There were places where remembering caused me to laugh and then there were places that brought me to tears. Then she shifted gears and began to give insight into what it takes to build a successful ministry, telling of the pitfalls you would undoubtedly face in the process. I was moved as she revealed the hurts you will experience while trying to keep a ministry growing. I would encourage anyone in ministry or even considering the idea of starting in ministry to read this book. I do know that the stories in this book and the reality of God's presence through it all are real, because we lived it. It's kind of funny now when we look back, but at the time we were not sure we were going to make it. However, God was always true to His word where He said, "I will NEVER leave you nor FORSAKE you." This is the word that we have lived by, and it has never failed us. Let me say, Ophelia has written a great book.

Prophet/Evangelist

Gary Ray

Endorsements

In the world we live in it is common to hear people talk about God in the general sense, but to know someone whose life is a testament to their relationship with Jesus is not common. I have been a witness to the evolving depth of that relationship between Jesus and my mom and can say that I know she intimately knows and trusts in our Savior, Jesus Christ. She has lived a standard of biblical truth before me. She has shown me how to be strong and fight without giving up, but she has also shown me what submission looks like. She has lived out what it means to be a woman of God.

I was so excited to hear that she felt called to write a book detailing her life and how God had a purpose for her and my dad to serve Him together in ministry. So much of their story I know because I lived it, however, reading the details from her point of view and in her voice gave me a new perspective.

I think this story is painfully honest but overriding all the pain is the beauty of redemption. Our God is an amazingly loving God, and I don't think it would be possible to read this and not recognize His love in every part of it.

As my dad's ministry developed and grew, I saw Mom's and Dad's relationship with each other and with Jesus grow with it and through it. What a legacy of sold-out service to God they leave me, my brother, and my sister. I will forever be thankful for them and for God's divine purpose that gave them to me.

Tiffany Ray Gentry

***

I had the privilege of reading my grandmother's book before it was published. What a wonderful book she has written. My grandparents have always been a strong Christian influence in my life. I learned so much about their ministry in reading this that I hadn't known before. This book is such a testament of deliverance, God's grace, and what it takes to make a ministry work. All different kinds of readers will benefit from this book. If you're planning to start a life in ministry, are interested in people's lives in full-time ministry, or just like a good book about life, you will love this book. As someone who has had the privilege to do life with the woman who wrote this book and lived the words on each page, I highly recommend that you go through this book and be prepared for what God will teach you through it.

Madison Gentry

First, let me begin by saying I have had the pleasure of knowing Ophelia and Gary Ray for over 18 years and I couldn't be more excited to share my thoughts about this book. Theirs is a story and ministry that is full of miracles, love, and struggle.

Ministry is often seen as a world full of respect and fulfillment. While that may be true some days, the largest part of ministry is selflessness and sacrifice. As you read this story told from the perspective of a minister's wife you get to see the real and the raw side of ministerial life. Ophelia Ray lets you inside the moments of their lives not often talked about. We always see the good side. The miracles, the prophecies, and the moves of God are all the joyous side of ministry, but no one sees the woman behind the scenes taking care of the children, paying the bills, managing the home and the ministry: the sacrifice that is being a minister's wife. Through this book, she opens up about the joys and the sorrows, the ups and the downs, the victories and the valleys. Ophelia shares it all and how God was always there to miraculously bring them through. I have rarely seen a woman more steadfast and loyal than Ophelia Ray. She is a true Proverbs 31 woman. She has taken her vows seriously to Gary and to God. Through it all, she has been the wind beneath his wings and the rock he could lean on. Together as a team they have reached countless souls and touched numerous lives. But it took two. No, three. Not just the man out front, but the woman holding it all together, and God in the center of it all. Every young pastor and his wife needs to read this book and understand that it's not a glamorous life, but at the end of the journey you can look back and marvel at God's hand.

Ophelia and Gary are the examples of what ministry should be. Loving people, loving God, loving each other.

Tiffany Sweeley

***

There are so few friends from whom we draw comfort and commitment that to recognize these attributes in a fellow Christian is rare. Having met the author almost at the very beginning of their ministry and having been very close to the family, I can emphatically attest to Ophelia Ray's gift of RADICAL hospitality, opening the door to all her other talents. I was there, traveling and sharing musically with their team when I knew she truly wanted to be a part of that with her beautiful singing voice. But, instead, she prayed, kept the home fires burning, mothered their children, and stayed focused on holding things together. Being loyal to that place, she meticulously cared for family and was a rock to her husband. Later as she was more freed to join him on the road, their journey took them places only partially mentioned in this book; and the depth of their attention to individuals whom they pastored is only skimmed over in her account here. I've observed Gary and Ophelia's 24-7 vigils during their congregations' various everyday burdens, realizing that much of their service was an offering, as is the nature of this calling.

They have pursued with excellence and unequivocal determination an unrelenting "discipling" of those they left behind as they moved on to their next assignment. The plight of this couple was many times quite vulnerable to discouragement. As one who has been around and very close to them on this journey, I can promise they have not fallen to defeat but have overcome the obstacles. I truly thought that Ms. Ophelia would rattle off story after story of their hilarious situations, as well as heart-touching circumstances and tragedies they have encountered along their way. Instead, she has produced a full project, introducing her loved ones, sharing the high points of their life, crisis and victories, and whetted our appetites for more. Hopefully, that will be another book. For this one, however, I sensed the Lord wanted her to pen more of what she gained spiritually from her obedience and dedication to His plan for them. That purpose is quite obvious with her inclusion of the Scriptures, which are paramount in her conclusions.

An understatement would be that she never misses an opportunity to be GRACIOUS in her responses to confrontations, and her gentleness is not simply an affront." She is genuine and a lady. The heart of Ophelia Ray has consistently sought the Lord Jesus along her life's path. Her refusal to give up through the trials has benefited all of us who have watched from the sidelines: the least of which was their baby girl's going on to heaven so much earlier than they would have ever conceived, and the sorrow they endured, yes, even until now.

Trust me, there is much to be admired in this selfless, never-give-up, compassionate friend. I hope you enjoy the sweet aroma of the beginning of her life with Bro. Gary, her incomparable quest to bless their children and their parents, and how after giving everything to the FATHER first, the rest has amazingly fallen into position and is still reaping a harvest.

So many have been affected by her life. I hope there will be a sequel to this great piece of herself, which is so honestly, interestingly, and humbly composed for others who are, or desire to be, shepherds of a flock. They are friends indeed, and she strongly resembles the Proverbs 31 woman.

Judy Potts

***

This book will show all who read it the goodness and mercy of God. It will also be a great tool for anyone who is in ministry or has a call of God on their life. As we read through this book, Karen and I were inspired and encouraged that we can make it through anything the devil may throw our way. Gary and Ophelia, this book will be a great blessing to all that read it. Thank you for allowing the Holy Spirit to use you to write this powerful book.

Evangelists Mark and Karen Poff

Kingsport, Tennessee

***

What an amazing journey my friend Ophelia has been on. To see the beautiful balance of her faith and trust in the Lord will truly encourage you.

No matter what kind of bumps or curves in the road she encountered on her journey, she knew the plans the Lord had for her life. Through all the hurt, pain, and many disappointments in her journey, the Lord always remained faithful. His glory shined so brightly through it all. Ophelia is a true woman of God that walks in His love. The power of His love has carried her through the perfect plan He has for her life. God's powerful and perfect love is still carrying her today. I highly recommend this book. The testimonies shared will encourage you as you go through life and the trouble and challenges it brings.

Charlotte Roff

Dedication

As I look back over the story this book tells, I can't help but realize what an important part our children played in this journey. Each one of them, in their own way, has filled a special place in this ministry.

Valarie, our oldest, has been a part from the very beginning. I learned early on what it was like to love a child that I did not give birth to. There was never a question as to whether she would be a part of our family.

Krispin, our second born, of course, wasn't with us but 46 days. I daresay she touched more people in her short life than most people touch in their entire lifetime. She was a fighter, and she taught her daddy and mama to have faith and hope and to accept God's will in everything, even though we didn't understand it at the time.

Tiffany, our third child, came into our lives one year after the death of Krispin. She came here with a bright personality, she always had a lot to say, and has in her adult years, been an encouraging and supportive force in our lives.

Dustin, our fourth and last child, came along after Gary was delivered from his addictions. After three girls, Gary was one happy man to learn that we had a boy! Dustin, along with the older ones, has paid a tremendous price for the ministry. They all lived a large part of their young lives without the presence of their dad. I found a card recently that Dustin had given to his dad one Father's Day when he was younger. He wrote in it, "Daddy, I want you to come home and stay."

Because of all the sacrifices you all have made for this ministry, I dedicate this book to you, Valarie, Krispin, Tiffany, and Dustin. You are loved and appreciated more than you know.

Introduction

God has dealt with me about writing this book for several years. I have never felt capable of putting into words the things that I wanted to express to those that read this book, so that they may be encouraged in ministry. Working in ministry (and it is work) requires a commitment like no other. People in ministry must be thick-skinned and determined to stand firm on God's Word. After all, we are all human, and we all make mistakes and bad choices, but the good news is that when we do make mistakes, God is always waiting and willing to forgive us and love us unconditionally. He is a God of second chances.

It is the enemy's job to try to cause you to fail in your work for God. Therefore, it is so important that we stay in the Word and have a healthy prayer life. With these two tools implemented in our lives, we can and will be victorious in everything we do. If you feel called to do a particular job in ministry, expect Satan to show you all the negative aspects of that job. Sometimes the scariest thing that God asks us to do will end up being the greatest blessing and will build our faith the most.

The last chapter of this book outlines the things that God teaches in His Word that will make your ministry successful and pleasing to Him. If you are a young minister or are the wife or husband of a young minister, keep in mind that the road of ministry is sometimes hard, and it demands sacrifice and commitment, but it is fulfilling and rewarding. Spend time studying and preparing for ministry. I can promise you that the result will be victory!

Ophelia Ray

Chapter One

Let me paint a picture for you of mine and Gary's up-bringing and how we arrived at the place in life that brought us together.

Gary was born on January 9, 1943, and raised in Tulla-homa, Tennessee. His parents were Aubrey B. (Buddy) and Lorayne Smith Ray. He is an only child. His dad was a Baptist minister. His great-grandfather built and started the church that Gary grew up in, Raysville Bap-tist Church in Moore County, Tennessee. Gary is a sev-enth-generation preacher, with six generations of preachers before him. They were all of the Baptist faith, however, and Gary was the first one of the Pentecostal faith.

Gary was saved in a revival at the age of twelve years old. He spent four years serving in the U. S. Navy. He came out of the Navy with a desire to sing southern gospel music and sang with various groups in the area until he and his cousins started their group, The Royals. That group consisted of Gary, his two cousins, Jerry and Andy, and a friend of Gary's, Jim Haley. The Royals were together when I met him in Nashville, Tennessee. Even though he knew he was called to the ministry at the age of twenty-one, he used his love for music to try to replace that call. As you will see later in this book, that did not work.

I was born Brenda Ophelia McDowell on October 10, 1950, to Lewis and Mae Minton McDowell on Cagle Mountain, a small community in Sequatchie County, Tennessee. I am the youngest of five, two boys and three girls. My dad was a nurseryman, and my mom was a homemaker. They believed in working hard, and their priority in life was putting God first in everything. Even though my dad was a very successful businessman, they lived a simple life, and our home was always very peaceful. I was raised in church from the time I was born. Even though I was too small to remember, my dad had a big log truck, and when church time came, he would gather up our neighbors until he filled the large bed of that truck, and he would take them to church. My dad's dad was a "circuit rider" preacher. He traveled by horse many miles on a regular basis preaching the gospel. We attended a Congregational Methodist Church until I was sixteen years of age. After that, we went to a Baptist Church until I left home for Nashville to attend business college. My dad also had a love for gospel music. We attended any or all singings that we could drive to every weekend. Even at that point in my life, God was instilling in me a love for the major thing that Gary and I had in common when we met. We even knew a lot of the same people in southern gospel music.

I was saved at a church camp in Lawrenceburg, Tennessee when I was twelve years old. I believe that the way I was raised and the "stickability" that I was taught growing up prepared me for the life that God had planned for me.

Chapter Two

I went to Nashville four months after I graduated from high school, in the fall of 1968. I wanted to get a quick education in business and office education, in order to become independent as soon as possible. My parents paid for my business college course and a place for me to stay that was within walking distance of the college since I didn't have a car. The place they chose for me to stay was a boarding house for girls attending school and working single girls that did not have cars. It was owned by the Central Church of Christ and operated by widows and single women from the church. It was an old, three-story brick house next door to the Greyhound Bus station. This was very convenient since I rode the bus home a lot of weekends. By bus, the trip home to Cagle Mountain took approximately three hours. Most of the rooms were double rooms, but I was fortunate enough to get a single room. It was furnished with a twin bed, a desk, and a metal locker. Everyone on each floor shared a common bathroom, which had showers. We had two meals a day furnished in the price of the room and board, which was $16.00 per week. They were prepared by two precious African American ladies that I learned to love very much. One of them was named Fannie, and I can't remember the other one's name. After all, that has only been fifty years. Yes, I said 50 years.

After I had been at the boarding home for about six weeks, one of the ladies that ran the place came to me and asked me if I would be interested in staying downstairs in the office and answering the telephone and doorbell until 7:00 in the evenings and every other weekend. (Because we were located on Fifth Avenue and Commerce Street we kept the doors locked and whoever was on duty had to unlock them for those coming in.) I gladly accepted the offer, because I thought that would help my parents financially.

For the record, the course that I had chosen to take (Medical Secretarial) was supposed to take nine months to complete. Students could finish at their own speed. I finished in seven months.

Little did I know that I would meet my future husband there. In fact, he had been dating a friend of mine that lived there. He came to get her one night, but she was in bed sick. Being the social person that he is, he asked me to go across the street for a cup of coffee after I got off work. We found out that we enjoyed a lot of the same things. I can't say that it was love at first sight, but there was something that drew us together from the first conversation that we had. Looking back, I think I knew from that first night that we had a future together.

We are opposites in almost every way. I am a planner—he is spontaneous. I am an organizer—he is very unorganized. You might ask, why would God ever put two opposites together? Balance is the ultimate goal and that sometimes leads to controversy. Believe me, we have had our share. God knew it would take balance to accomplish His plan for our lives. I can tell you that even after forty-seven years together, we are still opposites. If Gary and I had known the hardships and stumbling blocks that the enemy would put before us, we might not have been very excited about the journey ahead.

Chapter Three

We were married on April 12, 1971. We had our first child the day before our first anniversary, April 11, 1972. Gary had a daughter from a previous marriage, who was five years old when we married. Her name was Valarie Lynn. She had stayed with his parents since her mother abandoned her, and Gary had no one to watch her while he worked. He also lived in a boarding house in Nashville. Her mother did not contact her for thirteen years from the time she left her. When I was carrying our first baby, my doctor got my due date confused, and he induced my labor at eight months. Of course, I trusted him since he was a specialist in the OB-GYN field of practice and supposedly had a very good reputation in Nashville. The baby, who we named Krispin Nichol, weighed 5 lbs. 3 oz. when she was born. She was born at the time of development that her lungs had no lining; therefore she could not breathe long term on her own. One health issue led to another. She contracted Pseudomonas, and her heart was not strong enough to work through the health issues. Our pediatrician got her admitted under the hospital's study program (Vanderbilt is a teaching hospital). We will always be grateful for the team of doctors and nurses who took care of her during her stay there. For instance, Gary and I always went to the hospital late at night to check on her, since we weren't allowed to stay with her. One night we went, and we couldn't find a doctor to get an update on her condition. We went down the hall where the lab was located and found her doctor there drawing his own blood to give to her. The hospital didn't have any of her type, so he was making sure she had blood. That warmed our hearts to know that she was getting the best care possible. We learned a lot during her stay about the babies in the NICU. There were babies there that had been there weeks and weeks, and no one had been to visit them, including their parents. The doctors told us that it had been proven that the babies who had parents visit them regularly made faster recoveries (if they recovered at all) than those that had nobody that cared. Love does matter. She lived 46 days but was never well enough to come home from Vanderbilt Hospital.

Chapter Four

Of course, we were devastated! We could not understand why God would take her. I don't think it ever
crossed our minds to be angry at God. Although we
were hurt deeply, we had a peace because we knew it
was all a part of God's plan. We realized, many years
later, that He would use us to minister to couples that
had lost children. If we had not experienced the pain of
losing a child, we could not have been sympathetic to or
felt the pain that those we ministered to were feeling. It
became plain to us why God would allow her birth and
death. Even at this early time in our relationship, God's
plan was beginning to take shape in our lives.

We also knew that with all the health problems she was
dealing with because of her premature birth, if she had
lived, the possibility of her being blind, because of the
near 100% oxygen she had been on since a few hours
after birth, was great. Also, the doctors had prepared us
for the possibility of her having some severe mental

deficits. I must be perfectly honest with you, Gary and I had gone to that hospital and looked at her with 9 or 10 tubes in her at a time. As a mama and daddy, we could not bear the thought of the struggle her life would be if she had to live with severe mental deficits, blindness, or other problems. If she could not live and have a good quality of life, we did not want to be selfish and keep her here. We do have the assurance of seeing her again one day, and we know that she is whole and free from all the things she could have dealt with here. I am sure there were people who judged us for being relieved that she went on to heaven, but all I can say is, "don't judge until you have been in our position." Even though the whole ordeal was so painful to us, we realized that she got her healing, and heaven is sure sweeter because she is there.

Chapter Five

April 27th, 1973, our second child was born. Tiffany Danielle Ray arrived healthily, and she was definitely a unique little girl. She quickly filled the empty spot in our lives that had been left by Krispin. She could talk before she could walk and whole sentences I might add. We knew she certainly was sent to us with a lot to say! When Tiffany was two years old, Valarie came to live with us. I was "Mama" to her from that day forward. Even though there were times when Valarie suffered from the rejection of her mother, I never regretted taking her and raising her as my own. Tiffany married her husband, Mike, and we learned to love him like our own. They have two children: Madison, who is now 22 years old, and Jathan, who is now almost 18. Both of them are great Christian young people and very active in their church, First Baptist Church in Cookeville. Mike and Tiffany are great examples of what parents should be to their children. They never sent their children to church. They took them. I truly believe that pays off. "Train up a child in the way it should go, and when he is old he will not depart from it" Proverbs 22:6. Valarie has two children also. She has a daughter, Brittany, and a son, Zachary, who are both married and live in the Nashville area.

Chapter Six

Gary and his cousins had been raised in southern gospel music. Their Dads formed a quartet and traveled locally around Tullahoma, Tennessee, singing at homecomings and churches. The boys had gone with them and began their own group as soon as they were big enough to sing. It was in their blood, and it was all they knew. In 1969, they bought their first bus, such as it was, nick-named it Thumper, and hit the road. During the duration of their time singing, they owned three buses. Their group, The Royals, traveled and sang until 1974. Jim Haley was the only one of the group that wasn't related. He sang tenor for the group until the original group disbanded.

It was virtually impossible to make enough money to feed everyone's families by staying on the road. The wives of the group became a close group of women. Times were so hard that we would have to pool our food on weekends while the boys were on the road singing in order to feed our families. We didn't really mind, though. We always had enough to feed our families. The group definitely had the talent to make it, but the demand that it put on the families was more than they could sacrifice. In 1974, Gary began driving the bus for country music legend Kitty Wells and her husband, Johnny Wright. I'm sure the experience he had from driving the Royal's buses helped him land this job. He drove for them two different times, for a total of about three and one-half years.

Chapter Seven

Between 1974 and 1980, Gary drove for such country and rock groups as The Gatlin Brothers, The Oak Ridge Boys (while they were both gospel and country), AC-DC, Ted Nugent, Gary Wright, The Commodores, and The Jacksons. I'm sure this sounds like a dreamy and glorious career. The downside to this was that he developed a drug habit that would eventually threaten his life. He would be gone from home, sometimes as long as three months at a time. As his habit progressed, I saw less and less of his paychecks. I was at home working, taking care of our house, and raising our two girls. When he did make it home from a tour, he would be in such a terrible state that he would literally sleep for days at a time. As soon as he recovered from that run, he would leave on another tour, where he would do it all over again.

Because of the toll that this habit was taking on his body and our marriage, I made the decision to take our girls and leave, or to ask him to leave. When he saw that I was serious, his first reaction was to get mad, curse at me, and attempt suicide. Fortunately, our oldest daughter and I took the gun away from him and took it out of the house. I told him if he was going to continue on this road, that we were not going to stay and watch him die. He wasn't far from death. He had lost tons of weight, his teeth were rotted out, and he could not drink carbonated drinks because they would run out his nose. He quickly decided he was ready to get help. I'm not talking about him going somewhere to dry out or seek man's detox programs. The only help I could offer him was spiritual help. I offered to pray with him. He said he didn't think God would help him. I told him I thought it was worth a try. We knelt in our living room floor, and he cried out to God to come to him at that moment. God miraculously healed him. He never took another drug, never smoked another cigarette (that was a bonus), and he never drove another tour. Gary had gone so far away from God that he could not fulfill the plan that God had for him. Sometimes God lets us get so far down that we can't help ourselves in order for us to remember that we have to call on Him. All the time, He is waiting for us to get to the point that we will let Him help us. When we get to the point that we no longer have the answers to our problems, He is always ready to take over our situation and fix it for us. All He asks is that we allow Him to work in us. He will set us back on the right track and let us continue His plan in our life.

Gary said that he was called to preach when he was twenty-one. He talked to an older preacher about the calling. The older preacher told him the call of God on his life was a serious thing and that he had better be sure he was really called. The conversation scared him so bad that he was afraid he had not really heard from God. He did not accept the call on his life until he was 42 years old. Do you understand now why Satan tried so hard to put all the glamorous things in front of him? Satan worked overtime to try to destroy him, so he would not do what God had called him to do. Romans 11:29 says, "For the gifts and the calling of God are without repentance." He never withdraws them once they are given, and He does not change His mind about those to whom He sends His call.

Chapter Eight

When Gary came off the road and was delivered from all his addictions, he told me to gather all the tour shirts he had acquired from all the tours he had done and destroy them. He was so determined to not go back to that lifestyle, that he didn't want anything there to remind him of where he had been. I dare say he had 50-75 shirts with various band names and tour names on them. We later found out that some of them were worth quite a lot of money. I took them to my mom and dad's house and gave them to my sister that lived with them to use for dust rags. She put them upstairs and vowed to look at them when she had time. I never asked about them again. After my parents both died, I went to the house to help her clean out some of the almost sixty years of collecting papers, etc., they had stored upstairs in their house. Tiffany, our daughter, went with me to help clean. She found the shirts still in the bag, never touched. She asked to take them home with her. She cut the shirts and made her dad a quilt to use as a tool to show people where he had been. A picture of the quilt she made him is on the cover of his DVD which has his testimony on it.

Chapter Nine

Soon after Gary was delivered, we started going to a small Baptist church in the community where we lived. It had an attendance of 25 to 40 people most of the time. Gary understood that the safest place for him to be after his deliverance was in church surrounded by Christian people. He knew if he continued driving buses or spending time with the same people that had supported the habit he had, he would probably end up back in the same condition he had been in. After he made the change, or should I say after God made the change in his life, he did not hear from one of those people that he had associated with while he was doing drugs. We made some lifelong friends at this church and began our journey together in church as a family. For the next three or four years, Gary worked for a couple from Rodantha, North Carolina who owned a photography company. Their photographers traveled a designated area for a week at a time. They would be in groceries, 5 and

10's, or drug stores for a few hours on a scheduled day and take pictures of people. They sold a rather inexpensive package of pictures. Most of the pictures he took were of children. He eventually went into business for himself, and his parents scheduled the shootings and delivered the finished pictures.

Chapter Ten

In July of 1984, God blessed us with our third child. Dustin Forrest Ray was born on July 29th. We were beyond elated to have a boy! Gary had so wished for a boy that he would not even let me look at girl's baby clothes when we would go shopping for baby things. We are so proud of the heart that Dustin has, and the man he has become.

Our oldest daughter, Valarie married her high school sweetheart when Dustin was three weeks old. She had graduated from high school and turned 18 that same summer of 1984.

We met the Youngs from Spencer, Tennessee at the beginning of that year. They had a family singing group and sang all around Middle Tennessee. They consisted of Earl and Jane Young, and their only child, a son, Earl. The entire family was very musically talented.

They owned a music store which supplied most of the churches in the middle Tennessee area with sound systems, pianos, and any other music-related items that they needed. Gary and I joined their group and sang with them for several years. Jane and I became the best of friends. We spent many nights talking on the phone for hours. I considered her one of my three best friends.

On New Year's Eve of 1984, we were invited to sing for a church dedication at a little country church, Christian Fellowship Church, which was located on the Smithville highway out of Sparta, Tennessee.

Chapter Eleven

We immediately felt at home there and settled into Christian Fellowship Church. We called it home for the next eight years. Christian Fellowship Church was a full gospel, Independent Pentecostal church. This was a big change for us since as I said before, I was raised Methodist and Gary was raised Baptist. This is where we first learned about and experienced Pentecost. Gary accepted the call into the ministry in this church and was ordained there as well.

The pastor there, Brother George Haston, was in his seventies at the time. He mentored Gary, along with about 15 other preachers. He and his wife, Hazel, lived in a beautiful log house that he and his sons had built. Gary spent many hours in his home picking his brain and discussing the Bible. He attributes his foundation in ministry to this pastor.

During our tenure at Christian Fellowship Church, Gary made four trips to Jamaica. He helped build and establish three churches there. One of the more notable things that we were involved in while there was that we held a vacation Bible school there while we were youth pastors. We asked the pastor if we could undertake a vacation Bible school, and he said the church had never had one. He didn't believe there was enough interest in the church to make it successful. But he gave us the go ahead if we wanted to try it. We advertised it in town and offered to transport children to it. The first night we had around fifty attend. By the last night, we had over a hundred children in attendance. God really made it happen! I Chronicles 16:8-12 says, "O give thanks to the Lord. Call on His name; make known His doings among the peoples! Sing to Him, sing praises to Him; meditate on and talk of all His wondrous works and devoutly praise them. Glory in His holy name; let the hearts of those rejoice who seek the Lord! Seek the Lord and His strength; yearn for and seek His face and to be in His presence continually! Remember the marvelous deeds which He has done, His miracles, and the judgments He uttered." In other words, always give Him praise for what He is doing through you. Praise Him continually, and look to Him for His strength and guidance in everything you do.

Chapter Twelve

Gary spent the next eight years evangelizing, from Florida to Canada. I was not privileged to be a part of his traveling and ministry. At the time we had Tiffany and Dustin at home. It was necessary for me to work in order to pay our bills. This may come as a complete surprise, but unless a minister has the financial support and backing of an established church, it is virtually impossible to support a family with what one would be given through evangelizing. Therefore, I had to work a full-time job. That is not to say that some churches didn't take care of ministers that came to their churches, but lots of them felt no responsibility to do so.

In 1989, God began to speak to me to make preparations to move. He did not tell me where we would be moving, only to get things in order. I had worked at Townsend Engineered Products in Spencer, Tennessee for ten years. The Company had moved to Tennessee from Michigan in 1982. I was hired to establish and operate the purchasing department. I worked with a great group of employees, and I enjoyed my job. The one thing that troubled me was learning that this company did not want to promote women to positions of authority. There was no higher position I would be allowed to move into, so I really felt like things were working out as they should, and it was time for me to move on. We put our house on the market in Sparta, Tennessee. It sold quickly, and we moved into a rental house in town. We lived there for about three years until 1992. Gary had held revivals in the Tampa area of Florida over the years. One of the churches in Brandon, Florida had lost its pastor. We had become good friends with some of the people that were left in the church. They called Gary and asked him to pray about coming to Brandon, establishing a church, and being their pastor. That particular church that had left them without a pastor was a Pentecostal Holiness church. Gary was independent, so he was not at liberty to move into that building. After we prayed about the move, I was the one who felt the strong nudge to go to Brandon and begin a new church. The people there were in agreement that we come and begin a new church. God does not only speak to the preacher about decisions to be made when he is in a marriage. He confirmed the move to me also.

Chapter Thirteen

We moved to Brandon, Florida in May of 1992. One area where we saw God working this situation out was the way we found a house. Gary went down in the first part of April to start working on getting the church organized and ready to go. He had also preached revivals in a Puerto Rican church in Seffner, Florida, which was close to Brandon. The pastor agreed to let us have our services in their church until we could build up our numbers and be able to afford to pay rent on our own place. A lady that we did not know had shown up at the mid-week church service. Gary introduced himself, and she told him she was in real estate. He told her we were going to be looking for a house. I went down about three or four weeks before we were to move our household items down, and we began looking for a house to live in. When I got down there that weekend, she had a house lined up to show us. We did not plan to buy a house right away. After all, preachers of small churches usually can't afford to buy or even rent expensive houses. The house she showed us was a nice, three-bedroom, two-bath house that had been empty for a few months. The owners, an elderly oriental couple, had bought a doublewide mobile home in a senior community where the grounds were kept for them. The house was a stucco -covered house with three bedrooms, two baths, and a garage that had been enclosed and could be used for an office. We rented the house for $650.00 a month, with the option to buy after a year. The lady who owned the house had been in real estate. She knew the market value of rental properties and was hesitant to let us rent the house at the price we had wanted to pay. She later told us she didn't know why she let us have the house at that price, but we knew why. That was just another way God worked on our behalf, so that His plan would be fulfilled. A year later, we approached them about buying the house. They asked for a down payment of $5,000.00. Of course, on the salary our small church was paying us, we could not afford a down payment of that amount. We told them we would have to pass on buying the house and got ready to leave their home. She got up and started down the hall. She turned around and came back and said, "I don't know why, but we are going to let you have the house with no down payment." We knew why, even though she didn't. This sweet couple was Catholic, but God will use anybody that will let Him. The house was very comfortable for us, and we lived in it until we moved back to Tennessee.

For our first church service, we had seven people attend. During the next four and one-half years, our church body moved three or four times. We always improved our facility.

During this time of ministry, we experienced many miracles of God as well as some touching and heart-breaking moments. Here are just a few of the more notable experiences that come to mind.

Gary performed a wedding for two of our members. It was very unusual, in that the bride and groom were step-brother and sister (no blood kin) in a blended family of twenty children. They were both attending our church at the time of the wedding. They asked if Gary charged a fee for performing a marriage ceremony. He told them he did not, but they were welcome to give him a love offering if they wanted. On the evening of the ceremony, after it was over, Gary came out to our car for us to leave. He started pulling rolled coins out of his pockets and explained to me that the couple had graciously given him $42.00 in rolled coins.

Another unique occurrence was that he preached a funeral for a young man that had been killed in an auto accident. The young man's girlfriend sat with her friend and talked and laughed during the entire funeral, while their two small boys sat alone a couple of seats behind her and cried in heartache. His body was being flown to Texas after the funeral to his family for burial. Rather than go to the airport and see the body depart, the girlfriend chose to go out and eat with her friends.

Gary visited the AIDS floor of St. Joseph's Hospital in Tampa on a regular basis. A lady that attended our church had a close friend whose son, his wife, and both of their children all had tested positive for AIDS. Her son had contracted this dreaded disease from a "girlfriend." She had already passed away when Gary was sent to visit him. He had spread the disease to his wife, and ultimately to their two kids. Gary led him to the Lord before he died. When Gary held his memorial service at our church, he had an opportunity to minister to his family and friends. This family was all largely unsaved.

We experienced several "firsts" while we pastored in Florida. The people, in general, other than our core base of people that God had placed with us, were what we would consider unchurched. We learned a lot about dealing with those people as we tried to teach them about the love of Jesus, and what He expects of us as Christians. My husband made himself and our home available twenty-four hours a day, seven days a week, to anyone that needed him as a pastor. I do want to give credit to a few very faithful, dependable people who were with us from the very beginning to support us in anything we attempted to accomplish. They were also very supportive with their finances. We know that God placed them with us for that very reason.

Chapter Fourteen

We did not get to be with our families for holidays for the four years while pastoring. It was very hard to be away from our families on Thanksgivings and Christmases. Our daughter got married in Tennessee during this time as well. It was hard to feel disconnected from family, but God provided people in our church to be like family for us during this time. It was especially hard on our son, Dustin, who was a pre-teen by now. He loved his sister and missed her terribly. When we accept God's call into ministry, we rarely ever think of the sacrifices that we will have to make in order to serve in that call. Not only does the "minister" make the sacrifices, but his or her whole family makes the same sacrifice that they do. That is one reason why I think God wants a husband and wife to be equally yoked. In our situation, if I had not been a Christian or had wanted to do something entirely different with my life, I would not have been understanding when God told us to go to Brandon, Florida to begin the work that he wanted started there. Couples who are not in agreement where ministry is concerned, the success rate of that ministry will be low.

While we were in Florida, a group of doctors in Tarpon Springs had perfected an eye surgery to correct a person's vision. Gary went to them and had the surgery done. Things went wrong, and he ended up having a dozen or more surgeries trying to correct the problem. We moved back to Tennessee during all this, but they finally came to the conclusion that the eye had been operated on so many times that it was dead, and the only thing to do was a cornea transplant. We flew back to Tarpon Springs in 1997, and the transplant was done.

Chapter Fifteen

In January of 1996, our daughter was getting ready to give birth to her first child. Of course, she wanted us to be there for the birth. We wanted to be with her and her husband for this joyous occasion. We left the church in the hands of the elders. We were in Tennessee a week and a half for our granddaughter's birth. While we were in Tennessee, one of the elders got in the pulpit and told the people that he felt it was time to get a new pastor. This is the same elder that came to Gary before we left Brandon for Tennessee and gave him his gas cards to buy the gas to make the trip home. He hugged Gary's neck and told him he had learned more under his ministry than he had ever learned from any pastor. This obviously was a wolf in sheep's clothing. He totally destroyed the church. When we returned to Brandon, we had approximately twelve to fifteen people left out of about fifty. The people who were left were basically the same core group of people that we had begun with. We did not have enough people left to pay rent on a church building. We had services in our home on Sunday morning for the next several months. Gary spent a lot of that time very depressed, trying to make a decision about what we were to do concerning the church. In Psalm 42:5, the discouraged psalmist says, "Why, my soul, are you downcast? Why so disturbed within me? Put your hope in God, for I will yet praise him, my Savior and my God." Discouragement destroys hope, so naturally, the devil always tries to discourage us. Without hope, we give up, which is exactly what the devil wants us to do. Gary was discouraged and thought he had let God down, but he was not the one who destroyed the church. God did not punish him, even though Gary spent some time being depressed and felt like he had failed. He was not responsible for what the elder did that caused the breakup of the church.

We came home to do a benefit for a dear friend of ours that was battling cancer. This is the same man that had sung tenor for The Royals from their inception. During our time here, we made the decision to move back to Tennessee. Gary and Dustin stayed in Tennessee that trip, and I went back to Brandon to wrap things up, pack our house, and work out a notice on my job. I put our house on the market, and it sold within a month. We didn't know how we would rent a truck to bring our belongings back to Tennessee or cover any other expenses we would incur on the move. When we closed on the house there, we received a check for $5,000.00. God had supplied the necessary finances for us to make the move. We were bruised and hurt from the things that had tran-

-pired there. Gary questioned his decision to leave Florida and come back to Tennessee. He still feels like he
gave up too soon, instead of staying and seeing what
God would have done. I don't think there is one of us
who, somewhere along our journey, haven't felt like we
missed God. Just because we sometimes make a bad decision concerning ministry, it doesn't mean we just give
up and quit. God's grace is sufficient to forgive us and
help us get back on our feet again so we can continue to
follow His plan for our lives. When our children make
mistakes, we don't turn our backs on them and walk
away. We pick them up and love them unconditionally. God loves us just as much and even more.

When we returned to Cookeville, we did not have a
place to live, and we really didn't even know what we
were going to do from that point forward. We have a
couple of dear friends that lived in Cookeville that we
had gone to church with at Christian Fellowship Church
back in the eighties, Ray and Dot Brown. They had been
to Florida to visit us several times while we were there
pastoring. They reached out to us and offered us a place
to stay in their home until we could decide what we
were going to do. We stayed with them for about three
months. Rather than wear our welcome out, we moved
and stayed with another family that we had been close
friends with since our days at Christian Fellowship in
Sparta, Tennessee. They were like our family and closer
than some of our family. We are Godparents to their
children. He and Gary were ordained at the same
time. We have been through a lot of "life things" to-

-gether. Some were good, and some not so good. I can honestly say we have never been mad at each other. That is the kind of friendship we have. We are still very close to this day. Danny and Crochia Rogers had several kids in their home (they kept foster kids), but they made room for us to stay there for about a month. We had been attending the Algood Assembly of God since we had come back to Cookeville. The church had a congregation of about 1,500 people. We felt led to get a meeting with the pastor and let him know why we were there. The pastor, Brother Eddie Turner, gladly agreed to see us. We told him our story about our church in Florida. Who better to understand our hurt and injury from church people than another pastor. I dare say that most pastors who have spent any length of time pastoring, have experienced some degree of hurt. I truly believe that God places people in our paths who understand the things we are going through. He asked if we had a place to live until we could get our own place. When we explained that we were staying with friends, he offered us a church mission house to live in for five months. The church had missionaries coming home from the mission field that would need a place to stay when they arrived. We graciously moved enough of our furniture in the house to live and began making plans to spend the holidays with our families. This would be the first year we would be home in four years. In appreciation for the church letting us use this house, I painted some of the rooms and papered the kitchen. That was the least I could do. That pastor helped nurse us back to spiritual health again from the bruising we had experienced in

Florida.

We attended the church in Algood as long as we lived in Cookeville, which was three and a half years. This was another lesson that God let us learn from our experience with our church in Florida. We truly learned about hurt from church people that we trusted. He also helped us learn how to rebuild our trust after we have been hurt. Some of these lessons are very painful, but God knew that we would come in contact with preachers and church members along our journey that would need ministering to. Gary began to book some preaching dates around the Tennessee area. His evangelistic boundaries began to grow. Psalms 23:1-4 tells us that, "The Lord is my Shepherd (to feed, guide, and shield me). I shall not want. He makes me lie down in (fresh, tender) green pastures; He leads me beside the still waters. He refreshes and restores my life (myself); He leads me in the paths of righteousness for His name's sake. Yes, though I walk through the valley of the shadow of death, I will fear or dread no evil, for You are with me. Your rod and Your staff they comfort me." When we feel that we have failed terribly or have been hurt by someone we truly trusted, God is always there to pick us up, brush us off, and set us on the right path again.

In the meantime, I went to work for Claire's, a company that carried costume jewelry and such for young people. Tiffany was managing their store in Cookeville and was instrumental in helping me get hired. The first store I managed was in Nashville at 100 Oaks Mall. I stayed there for approximately six months. I was driving an hour and a half from Cookeville to the store, which was very taxing. I took that store with the agreement that if a store closer to me became available, I would have first chance at getting it. The store in McMinnville became available, and the District Manager offered it to me. It was about a forty-five-minute drive for me. I stayed at the McMinnville store for about fifteen months. In the meantime, a new outlet mall had been built just off Interstate 40 in Lebanon, Tennessee. The District Manager called me and offered me the store at the new mall. I started there in June of 1999. We moved to Lebanon in January of 2000. I stayed at Claire's, not because I loved the job, but because Gary was evangelizing, and our finances were very unstable. I had already come to the conclusion that, if he was going to evangelize, I would have to work a steady job in order for us to pay our bills. That is another sacrifice that people who are in ministry have to make most of the time. When one person in a couple is called into ministry, God really doesn't call just one of them. He calls both to ministry together. When we marry, we become one. So why would He call just half of the couple and not the whole unit? I knew when our children were small that I could not travel with him. Once they were grown and out of the house, I did sometimes resent the fact that I still could not be a part of things with him because of the necessity to work, because lots of churches do not feel the need to take care of preachers financially.

Chapter Sixteen

Shortly after we moved to Lebanon, Gary decided he wanted to get his GED. Back in 1960, he and two of his cousins, and a friend he was growing up with, all joined the Navy. He never finished high school, so he never got a high school diploma. Ever since I had known him, he would get down periodically and feel inadequate to fill his calling because he didn't have a high school education. Satan takes any and every opportunity he can to try to discourage you by telling you that you aren't qualified to do what God has called you to do. He went to the GED office in Lebanon and signed up to start studying for his GED. Keep in mind, back in 1964, after he was discharged from the Navy, he had gone to Murfreesboro, Tennessee and took the test to get his GED. When he called to see if he had passed, the person he talked to told him he had failed the test. This only made him feel worse and less adequate to accomplish anything in life. The first night he went into the office to study for the test, the lady working there told him she had to go back and see what he needed to study first, and she left the room. Shortly she returned and told him he did not need to study at all. He had passed the test in 1964! Satan had held him back from having enough self-confidence to do anything worthwhile telling him he didn't have a high school diploma; therefore he couldn't accomplish anything. He participated in a graduation ceremony and marched with the class that had just finished getting their diplomas. He was so excited! Just knowing he had a diploma gave him a new surge of self-confidence that he needed to go forward.

Chapter Seventeen

In March of 2000, I accepted a new position at the Lebanon Mall. I became manager of a shoe store, Bannister Shoe Studio. It was owned by Jones Company, a very reputable corporation at that time. A few years later, the company changed the name of my store to Nine West. Then again in a few years, they changed it to Easy Spirit shoe store. I remained as manager until the store closed in January of 2012. I have often looked back on the twelve years that I managed that store and wondered what I accomplished during that time, other than keeping an immaculate store and building a good reputation with my customers. That was nothing to sneeze at, but as far as ministry goes, I didn't feel like I accomplished much. As one well knows, retail has a big turnover in its employees, and my store was no different. Most of the help are young school girls. If something comes up on a Saturday night, or if they get asked out on a date, responsibility to a job doesn't mean much. I lived my life at the store just like I lived it anywhere else. I did not realize that those young girls were watching me and how I lived my life. I have made three or four forever friends that worked for me. I still keep in touch with them. I got a message not long ago from a girl that I cannot remember telling me that I had impacted her life more than I would ever know. She told me I held responsibility for her being the person she is today. I had no idea. That is why it is so important to live your life the way you should live it at all times. You never know when someone is watching you.

Chapter Eighteen

Shortly after Gary graduated, he started school to acquire a degree in Christian Counseling. God opened this door through a good friend of ours, a pastor, who was having classes at his church. Gary received a Bachelor of Arts Degree in Christian Counseling from Calvary Theological Seminary in June of 2001.This accomplishment opened up doors for another field of ministry. God was fulfilling His plan for our lives. Not bad for a boy who had no self-esteem or self-confidence and didn't think he could even get a high school diploma! He did a lot of counseling in our home. Because of his experience with drugs and his deliverance, he was able to help lots of people who were going through the same things. He worked with a halfway house in Smyrna for a few years. He is now working with another one in Lavergne on a regular basis. This kind of ministry gives him a lot of fulfillment since he relates so well to the men and women he ministers to. Be assured that when you go through bad things in life and make mistakes, God will use your experiences to help other people because you can understand what they are going through.

Chapter Nineteen

Because of our love of southern gospel music, we decided to visit a church in Smyrna, Tennessee, whose pastor had sung with the Happy Goodman Family, a well-known group in the music industry for thirty years. We visited River of Life Assembly and thoroughly enjoyed the music there. They had an awesome choir at that time. We quickly decided that was where we wanted to call home and began attending regularly in 2002. When the pastor learned that Gary held a degree in Christian Counseling, he offered him a position on staff. The agreement was that Gary would not charge for counseling, but the clients were asked to give him an offering for the time he would spend with them. The church would match the offering he was given. Like so many promises that pastors make recklessly, their part of the deal never happened. When Gary approached the associate pastor as to why they were not fulfilling their promise, he told Gary that in order to do counseling in the church's name, he had to have a master's degree.

Just so the record is straight, Gary called the head of the school in Florida and asked whether that was true. The gentleman in Florida told him he was as qualified to do the job as anyone who had a master's degree. Gary just turned in his keys and ended what he was doing at the church. We did remain at the church until 2007.

Chapter Twenty

We decided to start having a service on Sunday after-noons at the Sleep Inn in Smyrna, Tennessee. We struggled with that for about five years. We did have some wonderful times there, and God blessed us because we saw Him move on different occasions. We just didn't have enough committed people to support a ministry. We don't always understand God's plan. If we don't see things happen the way we expect them to, we think we have missed God. Isaiah 55:11 says, "So shall My Word be that goes forth out of my mouth; It shall not return to me void but it shall accomplish that which I please and purpose, and it shall prosper in the thing for which I sent it." Even though we may not see what is accomplished, God clearly tells us if we are in His will, and we believe we were, His Word did what He intended it to do. In 2013, we returned to River of Life church and attended there until early 2016.

In February of 2009, Gary had gallbladder surgery and a

hernia repaired. In November of that year, he had another hernia surgery. In early 2010, he went for a colonoscopy. The doctor who did the test came out and told me that Gary's colon was full of polyps. He felt there was no alternative but to remove all of his colon except for 5 inches. Praise God he had enough left to reattach, so he did not have to have a colostomy bag. The surgeon that removed his colon said he had to remove all the mesh from his previous two hernia repair surgeries because of the risk of infection. He explained to me that the likelihood of Gary's insides falling down in his stomach was great without the mesh. Sure enough, within a few months, he looked like he was pregnant. We began searching for a doctor that was qualified to do a "stomach reconstruction." This surgery is a very extensive and dangerous surgery.

The only surgeon in Nashville who was willing to do the reconstruction surgery was at Vanderbilt Hospital. He opened him up, laid all his organs out, lined his stomach with pig skin, and put everything back in place. Gary spent nine days in ICU, but once again God brought him through this ordeal and restored his health.

Chapter Twenty-One

In May 2014, Gary began having severe headaches. After a couple of weeks of agonizing pain in his head and his face feeling sore, I took him to the emergency room at Vanderbilt Hospital. After some testing and doctors conversing, they told him they thought he had temporal arteritis. This is a disease where the arteries that run up the side of his face and into his head got infected. It can be very dangerous if not treated quickly and properly. In order to correctly diagnose the disease, we had to come home for a weekend and then go back as an outpatient for a biopsy of the arteries in his head. Two days later the professor of rheumatology there called him and told him to be in his office the next day at 12:00. He said the disease was "hot" in his body, which meant they needed to start treating it immediately. The danger of this disease is blood clots, blindness, strokes, and death. It is also supposed to stay in a person's body for up to three years at which time it leaves and never returns. We met with Dr. Sergent, and he started Gary on 60 mg. of ster-

-oids per day. Of course, this drug has so many bad side effects that he also put him on several other medicines to try to counteract the steroids. He stayed on the steroids over two years. The doctor then switched him to a monthly infusion for the last year. The three year period ended in May of 2017. One of the results, because of the massive amounts of steroids he was on, was spinal stenosis. This weakens the spine and joints. He will deal with all the damage from the steroids for the rest of his life. He gained 70 lbs. while on the steroids and suffered loss of vision.

Gary had to pretty much put his ministry on hold for three years. Nahum 1:7 says, "The Lord is good, a Strength and Stronghold in the day of trouble; He knows (recognizes, has knowledge of) those who take refuge and trust in Him." I believe we are wise to make up our minds ahead of time concerning what we will do when trouble comes. Let me encourage you to decide to be stable before trouble ever comes. Decide to stay in faith, and remain thankful for what God is doing in your life. When difficulties arise, keep praising Him, and do not ever give up. God desires to remove everything from our lives that does not bring Him glory. He sends the Holy Spirit to live inside us as believers, to be in close fellowship with us, and to bring conviction of our every wrong thought, word, or action. We must all go through the refiner's fire. What does that mean? It means God will deal with us. He will change our attitudes, desires, ways, thoughts, and conversations. Those of us who go through the fire are the ones who will bring great glory to God. All the sickness that Gary went through, I believe, was a fire that he had to go through. He could have easily thrown up his hands and given up, but God gave him the endurance to go through it.

Chapter Twenty-Two

When we went back to River of Life Church, Pastor Johnny Minick told Gary he would produce a video of Gary's testimony. Gary had felt for a long time that a video was in God's plan to enable him to use it as a tool to reach young people. He had not been in a position financially to make it happen. This was definitely a part of God's plan. The video tells about how Gary happened to get on drugs, many of the bands that he drove for, and how he was miraculously delivered from the addictions he had acquired. A good quality video is quite expensive, and it was not likely that we would be able to afford to make one. However, God used Bro. Minick to make it happen. We will be forever grateful to Bro. Minick for being obedient in making this happen. Many times people who are struggling with addictions will not go to a church to hear someone give their testimony or preach, but they will sit down in their home and watch a video.

Chapter Twenty-Three

In January of 2012, the store that I had managed for twelve years closed. The company had hired a new CEO. His idea was to downsize the company, which he aggressively did. I regret that I did not keep a journal of all the doors that God opened while I was there, which allowed me to minister to employees and even some customers. I am thankful to God that he afforded me the opportunity to witness for him. Don't ever forget that the people around you are watching how you live your life on a day to day basis. That is the best testimony you can give. I realized after the store closed that God had provided a mission field for me. I pray that I was the example he wanted me to be.

Gary had been working on a book since our move to Florida in 1992. He would work on it for a few weeks and put it aside. He titled it *Deliverance: The Final Release of the Church*. It is truly a picture of the condition of the church today. I certainly think God anointed him to write this book. It took him a total of twenty years to finish it. He finally published it in 2015. The book was another step in God's plan.

I also published a cookbook in 2003. I wanted to do this for my daughters so that they would have a preserved copy of all our family recipes. These two items, along with Gary's video, are valuable items that we sell on our product table to help finance our ministry.

Chapter Twenty-Four

In 2009, we helped Gary's mother sell her house in Tullahoma, Tennessee. We moved her to Smyrna, Tennessee. She bought a condominium two streets from us. We knew the tasks of taking care of her would be ours eventually since Gary is an only child.

His dad had passed away in 2001. He had chronic leukemia for several years. He got an infection in his bloodstream. The doctors amputated his leg and hip. He lived sixteen days after the surgery.

My mom and dad both passed in 2008. They were both 97 years young. God blessed their faithful living with many years and miraculously, after having 5 children and living 97 years, they didn't have to suffer the loss of a child before their deaths. My oldest sister, Doris, was never married. She lived with and took care of my mom and dad until they passed away.

In April of 2012, Gary's mom broke her hip. She had to have surgery. I cooked her meals and cleaned her house. Even though she lived only two blocks from us, it was very hard for me to cook her meals and carry them to her and keep her house clean. She soon learned she could not live by herself any longer. I spent that summer packing her things (again) and getting other things ready for an estate sale. We had a three-day estate sale the first week of August. We moved her to our home at that time. We had no idea just how our lives would change from that day forward. We were both in for a shock! She has now lived with us for five years (six years this August). She will be 95 this September.

The task of being a caretaker for someone you love and feel responsible for is the most stressful and taxing thing we have ever done. I worked part-time at first after she moved in with us. We then realized she needed someone with her most of the time. I quit my job in 2015. Gary had bought a motorhome to travel in for ministry. It was a blessing for him at his age to be able to take longer trips where he could stop and rest when needed. Since she has been with us, he doesn't feel that he can leave me here alone with her for long periods of time. She has a tendency to fall a lot, and I cannot lift her. Also, at his age, he doesn't feel safe traveling alone for long distances. Our life has been put on hold (again) as far as us ministering together. He is working in churches that are within short distances of home.

Chapter Twenty-Five

In late 2015, due to the fact that Gary had been sick for several years and the fact that his mother was beginning to fall more and need more care, I felt like we should move closer to our daughter in Cookeville. Honestly, I didn't know what was ahead for me as the caregiver for Gary and his mom. Even though Tiffany has a family and works full-time herself, and they are all very involved in their church, I knew she would be a support for me if I needed her. Gary agreed with me, and even though he probably would have never made that decision on his own, he knew that was what we really needed to do. It also put me less than an hour from my sister. It was my responsibility to take her to her doctor's appointments in Chattanooga periodically. I was two hours away from her in Smyrna, so the move was good for that reason also.

When I told our son the decision we had made, he said he would come to Cookeville too. I love the fact that our children love us enough to want to be close to us. That makes my heart happy! He married Ashley in October of 2016. They live a short distance from us. He now has a stepson, Max, who is eight years old.

Chapter Twenty-Six

On May 25th, 2017, I woke up very confused. I tried to log onto Gary's computer to check our bank account, but I couldn't remember the information that I needed to know to log in to the account. I couldn't tell him our address, my birthday, or anything else that I normally would have known. He asked me if I needed to go to the doctor, but I couldn't think enough to know. He had an appointment with his orthopedic doctor that afternoon around 3:00. I normally drove him to all his appointments, but I told him I would go with him and that he would have to drive. I knew something was wrong, but I couldn't pinpoint what. We went to his appointment, and as soon as he was finished, he brought me back to the Cookeville Regional Hospital Emergency Room. They determined that I had had a light stroke. I spent four days in the hospital while they did numerous tests. My blood had been low a week before when I had gone to my primary care doctor, but she had not determined why. The hospitalists began trying to find out if I was losing blood somewhere. A GI doctor was called in to do an upper GI before I left the hospital. He found that I had multiple ulcers. Another upper GI was done in July and another in December. This one showed a mass on the back wall of my stomach. The doctor did another one in January to try to dissect and remove the mass. It has tested benign, praise God, but he said it was growing rather fast and he thought it needed to be removed. In January, when he went in, he said it was too large to remove through my throat. I went to Nashville to the GI doctor that had found Gary's colon problem back in 2010. We had become friends with him through the years. He did another upper GI in January and agreed that he could not remove it through my throat. He had the surgeon in his group do yet another upper GI the following week and perform an intrusive ultrasound to determine exactly what kind of mass it was and what should be done about it. Keep in mind I was put to sleep six times in eight months. Although, the kind of anesthesia they use for the test is not as deep as what they would use to do major surgery to remove the mass. At that point, the two doctors conferred and decided that because of the risk of putting me to sleep for major surgery with my diabetes as a factor and the heart issues I have, they would prefer to just let it be at this point. They will check it again in six months.

You see, just because you make a commitment to serve God and live for Him, doesn't mean that you won't have any problems. They may not all be health issues. Some may be financial or even emotional, but God did prom-

-ise that He would be with us and never leave us.

Chapter Twenty-Seven

There are things that God expects of us as Christians and workers in His ministry. The following things are all important in order to fulfill His plan for our lives in ministry. Scriptures are from The Everyday Life Bible.

A. Galatians 1:1 "Paul, An apostle (special messenger) appointed not by or through any man, but by and through Jesus Christ (the Messiah) and God the Father, who raised Him from among the dead."

You aren't chosen based on your past.

Have you ever thought that God could not or would not use you because of your past? No one was more likely to feel that way than the apostle Paul, who tried to destroy the early church. However, he received God's forgiveness and recognized that it was God who gave him his ministry and authority. No matter what your past, God wants to use you too. We must realize that as soon as God begins to call you into ministry, Satan also begins to make you doubt your abilities and tries to make you think you really did not hear from Him at all.

B. Ephesians 1:4-5 "Even as (in His love) He chose us (actually picked us out for Himself as His own) in Christ before the foundation of the world, that we should be holy (consecrated and set apart for Him) and blameless in His sight, even above reproach, before Him in love. For He ordained us (destined us, planned in love for us) to be adopted (revealed) as His own children through Jesus Christ, in accordance with the purpose of His will (because it pleased Him and was His kind intent)."

You have been chosen.

One of the strongest desires human beings have is to be loved, to be accepted, and to feel that they belong. We want a sense of connection and belonging to something or someone. We want to feel valuable. We cannot be guaranteed of always getting that in our dealings with people, but we can get it from God. Even though He knows everything about us—and I do mean everything—He still chooses us on purpose. He actually picked us out on purpose to be His very own and to belong to Him. He set us apart for Himself and made provision in Jesus for us to be holy, blameless, and consecrated. We can live before Him in love without reproach. That means we do not have to feel guilty and bad about all our weaknesses and faults. You and I are no surprise to God. He knew exactly what He was getting when He chose us. He did not choose us and then become disappointed because of our inabilities. God be-

-lieves in us and is working in us to help us be all that He has in His plan for us.

C. Romans 8:31 "What then shall we say to (all) this? If God is for us who can be against us? (Who can be our foe, if God is on our side?)"

God is for you.

Even when we are obeying God to the best of our ability, we often have no natural way of knowing for sure whether we are right or wrong. We have nothing but faith to help us take that first step. Sometimes we may be wrong. If our hearts are right, and we do our best when we hear from Him, God will redeem us and honor our steps of obedience. If we move in trust to obey what we believe in our hearts that He has told us to do, even if that decision is wrong, God will take that mistake and work it out for our good. His word tells us that all things work together for good for those of us who love Him and are called according to His purpose. People who are too afraid to obey are so miserable anyway that they cannot get any worse off by stepping out and trying to do what God is telling them to do. Sometimes you have to step out to find out. You won't be the first person that either didn't hear from God or didn't hear what you thought you heard.

D. Galatians 1:15-16 "But when He, who had chosen and set me apart even before I was born and had called me by His grace saw fit and was pleased. To reveal His Son within me so that I might proclaim Him among the Gentiles as the glad tidings, immediately I did not confer with flesh and blood."

God's call to you.

Paul says that when he was called by God to preach the gospel to the Gentiles, he did not discuss the matter with anyone else. Many times when we receive a message from God, we confer too much with our friends and fellow ministers. We go around looking for someone to assure us that we are doing the right thing. What we need to do is realize that we have the Holy Spirit, or the Spirit of Truth, within us. But just because we have the Spirit of Truth within us, should we always shun the advice from others? No, Proverbs 11:14 says that in the multitude of counselors there is safety. Like many other things, this is an area in which we need balance. We can and should be open to receive advice from those who are wiser and more experienced than we are in a particular area, but we should not depend so much on what people say that we fail to obey what God is saying directly to us.

E. Mark 6:11 "And if any community will not receive and accept and welcome you, and they refuse to listen to you, when you depart, shake off the dust that is on your feet, for a testimony against them. Truly I tell you it will be more tolerable for Sodom and Gomorrah in the judg-

-ment day than for that town."

Shake off rejection.

Do not worry about what people think. If you do, you are going to worry all your life because the devil will never stop finding people who will think something unkind about you. When Jesus sent His disciples out into the towns to preach, He told them what to do if people rejected them. He did not tell them to stand around and cry and be wounded, hurt, bleeding, and embarrassed. He told them to "shake it off."

F. Luke 2:19 "But Mary was keeping within her all these things weighing and pondering them in her heart."

Learn when not to speak.

Whatever Mary may have thought or felt, she controlled it because she probably knew that if she shared the news with a lot of her friends, they would not believe her, and worse still, they would spread it to everyone they knew. I believe when God speaks something to us, many times we need to keep it to ourselves. This is especially true of prophets or pastors. Many times God speaks to those in leadership positions about someone under them so that they will know how to pray for that person. If you tell everything God has spoken to you about an individual, many times it will cause hurt and/or embarrassment. If that word travels back to the person, it will also cause distrust in you. You should have heard some of the things people said to Gary when he told them that God had called him into ministry. Knowing his background and the condition he had been in previously, they were not encouraging at all. People can be hurtful and judgmental. Especially "church people," who can be the most hurtful and judgmental people of all. If you do not fit into their mold of what they think you should be, they call you a failure before you start. Do not try to tell them you are a changed person. Let them witness the change that God has made in your life. This is one of the problems with sharing too much with others. We get discouraged instead of encouraged.

G. John 10:2-5 "But he who enters by the door is the shepherd of the sheep. The watchman opens the door for this man, and the sheep listen to his voice and heed it; and he calls his own sheep by name and brings them out. When he has brought his own sheep outside, he walks on before them, and the sheep follow him because they know his voice. They will never follow a stranger but will run away from him because they do not know the voice of strangers or recognize their call."

Learn God's voice.

People ask, "How can I be sure I am hearing from God?" The Word says we can know His voice and distinguish it from others. He gives us discernment to iden-

-tify His voice over voices of deception. In order to discern the difference between His voice and the voice of deception, we must know God's character, nature, and the history of how He has led others before us. We will know that what we have heard either lines up with His Word or contradicts His Word. To hear God and avoid not knowing His voice when He speaks, it is important to look into His Word and spend time with Him there.

H. Acts 6:2-4 "So the twelve apostles summoned the multitude of the disciples and said, it is not seemly or desirable or right that we should have to give up or neglect preaching the Word of God in order to attend to serving at tables and superintending the distribution of food. Therefore, select out from among yourselves, brethren, seven men of good and attested character and repute, full of the Holy Spirit and wisdom whom we may assign to look after this business and duty. But we will continue to devote ourselves steadfastly to prayer and the ministry of the Word."

Learn to distribute duties—You can't and shouldn't try to do everything.

As pastors or leaders in church, we should not try to be everything. We should select our roles cautiously so we can remain calm, cool, and steady in life. I firmly believe God provides for whatever He assigns to us. He will make sure we have all the people we need to help us, but it is not their fault if we will not rely on them. If you find yourself trying to do something and you do not have the help you need, you might need to ask yourself if you are doing the right thing. Why would God ask you to do something, then sit by and watch you be frustrated and miserable because the burden is too much? God meets all of our needs, including the people we need to work alongside us. If the apostles had not recognized their need for help, their priorities would have remained out of line and their true assignment unfulfilled. This is an excellent example for us to follow. Pastors should not try to fill all positions in their church themselves. Lots of times pastors will say, "I don't have anybody to be teachers, Sunday school superintendent, song leader, etc. I have to do it all." That position is better left unfilled until God sends the person He wants in the position, rather than the pastor spread himself so thin that he doesn't have time to study for messages and pray for the needs of the church.

I. John 16:7-8 "However, I am telling you nothing but the truth when I say it is profitable (good, expedient, advantageous) for you that I go away. Because if I do not go away, the Comforter will not come to you; but if I go away, I will send Him to you to be in close fellowship with you. And when He comes, He will convict and convince the world and bring demonstration to it about sin and about righteousness and about judgment."

Let the Holy Spirit work in you.

Jesus told the disciples that when the Holy Spirit came,

He would have a close relationship with them and would convict them of sin. The Holy Spirit guides believers into truths. Every time we get off track or go in a wrong direction, the Holy Spirit convicts us that our behavior or decision is wrong. If we are willing to cooperate with the Holy Spirit, we can grow into spiritual maturity and release all the blessings of God in our lives. If, however, we ignore the Holy Spirit's conviction and go our own way, we will find it very difficult. Our lives will not be blessed, and as a result, we won't bear fruit. I believe Satan's counterfeit for conviction is condemnation. Condemnation always produces feelings of guilt. When we are condemned, we feel under something heavy, which is what Satan wants. God, on the other hand, sent Jesus to set us free and give us peace and joy. As Christians, we should be light and carefree, not oppressed and heavy with burdens that we are unable to bear. Jesus came to bear our burdens. He alone is able to do that.

J. Romans 12:14-21 "Bless those who persecute you; bless and do not curse them. Rejoice with those who rejoice, and weep with those who weep. Live in harmony with one another; do not be haughty but readily adjust yourself and give yourselves to humble tasks. Never overestimate yourself or be wise in your own conceits. Repay no one evil for evil, but take thought for what is honest and proper and noble in the sight of everyone. If possible, if it depends on you, live at peace with everyone. Never avenge yourselves, but leave the way open for God's wrath; for it is written, vengeance is mine. I will repay says the Lord. But if your enemy is hungry, feed him; if he is thirsty, give him drink; for by so doing you will heap burning coals upon his head. Do not let yourself be overcome by evil, but overcome evil with good."

Let God avenge you.

Some people are basically impossible to get along with, but His Word says to do as much as you can to live at peace with everyone if at all possible. You cannot do their part, but you must do your part to keep peace with everyone.

K. Romans 12:11 "Never lag in zeal and in earnest endeavor; be aglow and burning with the Spirit, serving the Lord."

Stay on fire.

You may ask, "How do I stay on fire?" By the Word of God coming out of your mouth in the form of prayer, praise, preaching, or confession. These things fan the fire. They stir up the gifts within you, keeping the fire aflame. Whatever your hands find to do, do it with all your might. Stay active in the work of the Lord. Do everything you do for the Lord willingly and with your whole heart.

L. I Corinthians 12:31 "But earnestly desire and zealously cultivate the greatest and best gifts and graces. And yet I will show you a still more excellent way (one that is better by far and the highest of them all-love)."

Above all—Love.

Love is the greatest thing in the world, and it should be number one on our spiritual priority list. We should study love, pray about love, and develop the fruit of love by practicing loving others. Love is one of the nine fruits of the spirit available to those in whom God's Holy Spirit lives. God is love, so when we walk in His love, we abide in Him. Because we walk in God's love by receiving and expressing it to others, we should not deceive ourselves into thinking we can love God while we hate other people. Love not only blesses others; it also blesses the one doing the loving. Concentrate on being a blessing to others, and it will bring joy to you.

M. I Corinthians 15:41 "The sun is glorious in one way, the moon is glorious in another way, and the stars are glorious in their own way; for one star differs from and surpasses another in its beauty and brilliance."

Being different is okay.

We are all different like the sun, the moon, and the stars. God created us to be different from one another, and He did it on purpose. Each of us meets a need, and we are all part of God's overall plan. When we struggle to be like others not only do we lose ourselves but we grieve the Holy Spirit. God wants us to fit into His plan, not to feel pressured to try and fit into everyone else's plans. Different is okay; it is alright to be different. We are all born with different temperaments, different physical features, different fingerprints, different gifts, and abilities. Your goal should be to discover what you are supposed to be as individuals and then succeed at that. One of the biggest turn-offs to me is to go to hear a preacher, and as soon as he starts speaking, I realize he is mimicking another preacher. When we attempt to do what others are good at, we often fail because we are not gifted for those things, but that does not mean we are good for nothing. We should look for what we are good at and function in it. Secure people who know God loves them and has a plan for them are not threatened by the abilities of others. I would encourage you to enjoy what others can do and to enjoy what you can do. By thinking and saying positive things about yourself, you release the gifts God has in you.

N. Philippians 1:6 "And I am convinced and sure of this very things, that He Who began a good work in you will continue until the day of Jesus Christ (right up to the day of his return), developing that good work and perfecting and bringing it to full completion in you."

God will finish the work in you.

God always finishes what He starts. He has called us unto Himself and started a good work in us, and He will finish it. That is a promise. Of course, we have a part to play, which is to keep believing Him and cooperating with the sanctifying work of His Spirit in our lives. Jesus understands that sometimes we get in the middle of things, and we don't know how to go forward and finish His work. He understands that. Jesus lived in a fleshly body while here on earth, and He understands what it is like to be tempted. You may experience temptation or sin or even just give up and quit, but God will strengthen you all the way to the finish if you will ask Him. So many people start things and never finish them. That is not pleasing to God. In fact, that is not even a good representation of a person who desires to walk in integrity. It is easy to start things, because all of our emotions are excited about something new. But, character is seen in what people do when their feelings are no longer supporting them, and perhaps they are left alone with just God and a lot of hard work. Before you start anything, count the cost and make the decision that you will finish. God has promised to finish the work He started in you. You should make the same promise to Him to finish whatever He gives you to do.

O. I Timothy 3:1-12 "The saying is true and irrefutable; If any man seeks the office of bishop (overseer), he desires an excellent talk (work). Now a bishop must give no grounds for accusation but must be above reproach, the husband of one wife, circumspect and temperate and self-controlled; he must be sensible and well behaved and dignified and lead an orderly (disciplined) life; he must be hospitable (showing love for and being a friend to the believers, especially strangers or foreigners, and be a capable and qualified teacher. Not given to wine, not combative but gentle and considerate, not quarrelsome but forbearing and peaceable, and not a lover of money (insatiable for wealth and ready to obtain it by questionable means). He must rule his own household well, keeping his children under control, with true dignity, commanding their respect in every way and keeping them respectful. For if a man does not know how to rule his own household, how is he to take care of the church of God? He must not be a new convert, or he may develop a beclouded and stupid state of mind as the result of pride (be blinded by conceit and fall into the condemnation that the devil once did.) Furthermore, he must have a good reputation and be well thought of by those outside the church, lest he become involved in slander and incur reproach and fall into the devil's trap. In like manner the deacons must be worthy of respect, not shifty and double-talkers, but sincere in what they say, not given to much wine, not greedy for base gain craving wealth and resorting to ignoble and dishonest methods of getting it. They must possess the mystic secret of the faith (Christian truth as hidden from ungodly men) with a clear conscience. And let them also be tried and investigated and proved first; then, if they turn out to be above reproach, let them serve as deacons. The women likewise must be worthy of respect and serious, not gossipers, but temperate and self-controlled, thoroughly trustworthy in all things. Let deacons be the hus-

-band of one wife, and let them manage their children and their own households well."

You must be found faithful.

If we want to exercise authority, we must also know how to come under authority. We must learn to be faithful and stay wherever God has placed us until He moves us. We must respect and obey those in authority over us. We must do the right thing simply because it is right, even though we may never understand why, which is a real test of our faithfulness and obedience. The scriptures above tell us that a spiritual leader must live his life in such a way that no one has grounds to accuse him; he must be above reproach. In other words, he must behave so well that people cannot find any reason to blame him for wrongdoing. A leader must be hospitable and friendly, especially to outsiders. A leader must be a capable and qualified teacher. This involves teaching by example. People want to see Christians who live good, clean lives. It is our job to set a good example and pass along the principles of godly living to others. So many times I have heard sinners say, "I'm not going to church. I live as good as those so-called Christians do." And the sad part is, many times they do.

P. I Timothy 6:12 "Fight the good fight of the faith; lay hold of the eternal life to which you were summoned and for which you confessed the good confession of faith before many witnesses."

Fight the good fight.

To be a fighter is to be aggressive. We should fight the good fight of faith in our daily lives as we struggle against spiritual enemies in high places and in our own minds and hearts. One part of fighting the good fight of faith is the ability to recognize our enemies. As long as we are passive, Satan will torment us. Nothing is going to change about our situation if all we do is sit and wish things were different. We have to take action. Too often we do not move against the enemy when he comes against us with discouragement, fear, doubt, or guilt. We just draw back into a corner somewhere and let him beat us up. We believe his lies when we should stand against him with the truth of God's word. You and I are not supposed to be punching bags for the devil; instead, we are called to be fighters and respond aggressively to his attacks.

Q. James 3:8-10 "But the human tongue can be tamed by no man. It is a restless (undisciplined) evil, full of deadly poison. With it we bless the Lord and Father, and with it we curse men who were made in God's likeness. Out of the same mouth come forth blessing and cursing. These things, my brethren, ought not to be."

The power of the tongue.

The Bible says a great deal about the tongue and the

words of our mouths. The tongue holds the power of life and death. The apostle James said if any man can control his tongue he is a "fully developed character" and can also control his entire being. The tongue is a little member of the body, but it causes tremendous problems. Relationships often end because of things that are said or not said. People lose jobs, cause strife and misunderstanding, and embarrass themselves all with that one tiny organ, the tongue. We cannot tame our tongue by ourselves, so we need God's help. King David prayed that God would put a watch or a guard over his mouth. He also prayed that the words of his mouth and the meditation of his heart would be acceptable in God's sight. David knew he could not control his mouth without God's help, and neither can we. We can speak words of healing or words that wound; we can edify and build up or discourage and tear down. The decision is ours. Words are seeds that we sow, and they definitely bring a harvest in our lives. Those who indulge the tongue must eat the fruit of their words, whether they are for life or death. One thing we should do is think before we speak. The Bible says we are not to be quick to say things, but how many times do we speak and then think, "Oh, I wish I had not said that?" But then it is too late because the words are already doing their work. We should all pray that God would help us tame our tongue.

R. I Peter 5:8 "Be well balanced (temperate, sober of mind), be vigilant and cautious at all times; for that enemy of yours, the devil, roams around like a lion roaring, seeking someone to seize upon and devour."

Even in ministry, be balanced.

Maintaining balance in all things is so important. If we do not, we open a door to Satan, who roams around hungrily seeking to devour us. We should maintain the balance of work and rest, eat a balanced diet, never spend more than we earn, and enjoy people but also spend time alone. Although we want to please people and have their approval, we must put God and His will first in our lives at all times. If we do not maintain balance in our lives, Satan will take advantage of the door we have opened. This brings to mind when we moved to Florida to pastor, the people there that we were friends with were so happy we had moved there that they would all come to our house almost every night for fellowship, and lots of nights they brought dinner for everyone. They would stay until 10:00 or 11:00. This went on for weeks. Finally, Gary said to me, "I'm glad that they are proud we are here, and I love to fellowship, but this has gotten out of hand." Gary is a socializer and loves having people around him. He told them that we really appreciated their visits and the dinners they brought, but we needed to get our son in bed earlier than we had been, and we needed our rest also. He said this to them in love, and they understood.

S. II Thessalonians 3:5 "May the Lord direct your hearts into realizing and showing the love of God and into the steadfastness and patience of Christ and in waiting for His return."

Be patient with God.

Patience is not the ability to wait. It is how I act while I wait. You must wait with a good attitude. Waiting and not being happy about it is not patience. Our attitudes and actions during the wait determine whether we enjoy the trip and also help determine the length of the wait. There is a good reason that we need to be patient. We must deal with attitudes that hinder us, such as being jealous of others who already have what we are waiting for, having our own pity parties, riding an emotional roller coaster, and displaying all other kinds of bad attitudes. When God asks us to be patient, he is preparing us for something He is about to do in us or through us. Enjoy the wait!

T. Revelations 22:12 "Behold I am coming soon, and I shall bring My wages and rewards with Me, to repay and render to each one just what his own actions and his own work merit."

God's payday is coming.

Every person, with no exceptions, will one day stand before God and give an account of his life. Do not live like there is no tomorrow because tomorrow always comes. Jesus will come for us when we least expect it, and it will be too late to do all the things we intended to do but never got around to. We know that we reap what we sow. Our works are not judged by how much we did, or if we did them well or bad, but by the motives behind them. We need to make sure we are doing what we do with the right motives in mind.

The above twenty points that I have given you in order to have a successful ministry should apply not only to people called into leadership positions in ministry but to all Christians living for God. I speak these things from the standpoint of full-time ministry because that is what Gary and I have done for 34 years. I felt led to give you a "journal" of our lives to show you that ministers are just like everyone else. They are human with everyday problems, trials, victories. God has given us a roadmap to help us deal with and overcome the things we face on a daily basis. Our journey has been unique, in many ways, but we have not had one thing come before us that God hasn't been there to help us through. No, our lives have not been perfect by any means, but His mercies have been there every day to help us get back on the right track and continue on our journey. May we always be found living in obedience to God, fulfilling His plan for our lives.

For More Information

Contact:

Opheliamray@gmail.com

www.ingramcontent.com/pod-product-compliance
Lightning Source LLC
Chambersburg PA
CBHW060131050426
42448CB00010B/2073